PINOCCHIO

Carlo Collodi

WorldCom Edu

Adapted by **Lori Olcott**
Illustrated by **Kim Sook**

Copyright © WorldCom Edu 2003

Published in Korea in 2003 by WorldCom Edu

All rights reserved. No part of this publication may be reproduced, stored in a retrieval system, or transmitted in any form or by any means, electronic, mechanical, photocopying, recording, or otherwise, without the prior written permission of the publisher.

Printed and distributed by WorldCom Edu

작가와 작품 설명

카를로 콜로디(Carlo Collodi, 1826 ~ 90)는 이태리 피렌체 출신의 동화작가로서 본명은 카를로 로렌치니이다. 이탈리아의 독립 전쟁에 참전한 후 정치잡지를 창간해 애국사상과 독립운동을 고취시킨 인물이기도 하다. 이탈리아의 장래를 짊어질 아동들을 훌륭하게 길러야 한다는 사명감으로 아동문학의 집필에 전념했으며, 그 대표작이 『피노키오의 모험』이다. 이 작품은 지금도 전세계에서 널리 읽히는 명작으로, 그가 그려내는 공상의 세계는 확고한 사실주의를 바탕으로 교훈적이면서도 재미있는 내용의 이야기를 재치와 기지로 빠르게 전개시킴으로서 어린이들을 사로잡는다. 이 외에도 『요정 이야기』『지아네티노의 문법』등 전래동화를 새롭게 고쳐 쓰거나 교육적인 내용의 책을 집필하였다.

작품 설명

이 작품의 원제는 『피노키오의 모험』으로서, 목수 제페토가 만든 목제인형 『피노키오』가 게으르고 노는 것을 좋아하다가 험난한 모험을 하면서 스스로 뉘우쳐 착한 행동을 하고 남을 생각할 줄 알게 되어 진짜 사람이 된다는 내용을 담고 있다. 이 이야기는 단순히 교훈적인 내용에 그치지 않고 어른들이 아무리 아이들을 이끌어준다고 해도, 착하게 될 것인지는 어린이들 자신의 결단에 달려있다는 점을 아이들에게 일깨워 준다.

Introduction

Hello, and thank you for your interest in Worldcom's Story House! I hope you and your children enjoy the stories and characters we present to you here.

These Fairy tales have been passed down from parent to child for generations and generations. They usually teach a lesson. They teach the values that are important in every culture; like being kind, generous and helpful to others. They show that looks can be deceiving. Something beautiful, can be cruel and evil. But something ugly, can be good and loving. They also teach the value of patience. Rewards for good deeds don't always come quickly. But be patient, and the good deeds you do will bring good deeds to you. And if you keep working hard, your efforts will pay off.

I have tried my best to re-tell these stories in modern and natural English, without being too complicated or too hard. Most middle school children can read these stories. But I hope that parents and other adults will enjoy reading these books with their children too. There are interesting parts in each story. I hope there is enough that everyone will enjoy reading the story and listening to the native speakers.

Again, thank you for joining us in Story House. We hope you enjoy your stay.

이 책을 펴내며

안녕하세요. 월드컴의 Story House에 오신 것을 환영합니다. 부디 여러분과 여러분의 자녀들이 이 책이 들려주는 이야기들을 만끽하시길 바랍니다.

이 동화들은 부모에서 아이들에게로 여러 세대에 걸쳐 전해내려 온 이야기로서 교훈을 담고 있습니다. 이웃에게 친절하고 서로 도우면서 아낌없이 베푸는 것, 이러한 가치관의 중요성을 일깨워 주죠. 이러한 것들은 때때로 반대로 표현되기도 합니다. 겉보기에는 아름답지만 잔인하고 사악할 수 있으며, 비록 흉칙하게 보여도 착하고 사랑을 베푸는 사람일 수 있다는 것입니다. 이러한 이야기들은 우리에게 인내의 가치를 일깨워 주기도 합니다. 선한 행동의 대가는 그 즉시 되돌아오지 않습니다. 그러나 참고 기다린다면, 여러분의 선한 행동은 보답을 받을 것입니다. 그리고 열심히 노력한다면 그에 상응하는 결과를 얻을 것입니다.

저는 이 이야기들을 너무 복잡하거나 어렵지 않도록 현대적이고 자연스러운 영어로 전달하기 위해 최선을 다했습니다. 이 책은 중학교 수준의 학생이라면 누구든지 읽을 수 있습니다. 그러나 부모님을 비롯한 모든 이들이 자녀분들과 함께 이 책을 즐길 수 있기를 바랍니다. 이야기마다 제각기 재미있는 부분들이 있습니다. 네이티브들이 들려주는 생생한 이야기는 현장감을 더해 주어 자신도 모르는 사이에 동화세계에 빠져들게 될 것임을 믿어 의심치 않습니다.

다시 한 번 저희 Story House에 오신 것을 감사드리며, 계속 많은 사랑 부탁드립니다.

Lori Olcott

등장인물 주요 등장 인물

피노키오
나무로 만든 꼭두각시 인형. 말썽만 부리면서 제페토를 힘들게 하지만 험난한 모험을 거치면서 자신의 잘못을 뉘우치게 된다.

제페토
꼭두각시 인형을 만드는 노인. 인정 많고 따뜻한 마음씨를 가져 피노키오에게 아낌없는 사랑을 베푼다.

푸른 요정
위험에 처한 피노키오를 도와주고, 결국 갈 곳이 없어진 그를 애정으로 참을성 있게 돌봐 준다.

여우와 고양이
'기적의 들판'이라는 거짓말로 피노키오를 속여 금화를 빼앗으려 한다.

그 외의 등장 인물

  인형극 지배인과 마부

아이들

 그 외의 인물들
(서커스단 주인, 선원, 이웃)

Contents

Chapter 1   10
Comprehension Checkup I   26

Chapter 2   30
Comprehension Checkup II   56

Chapter 3   60
Comprehension Checkup III   86

Chapter 4   90
Comprehension Checkup IV   110

Answers   114
Word List   118

Chapter 1

Once upon a time, there was a puppet maker named Geppetto. Geppetto lived by himself in a village. His wife died many years ago. One day, he found a beautiful piece of wood. It was long and straight. He carved it with his knife. The wood carved easily.

This wood is perfect. I will make a new puppet with this wood.

once upon a time 옛날 옛적에
puppet 꼭두각시 인형
maker 만드는 사람, 제작자
live in …에 살다
by oneself 혼자서, 홀로
village 마을
many years ago 오래 전에

one day 어느 날
find(-found-found) 찾다, 발견하다
straight 곧은
carve 조각하다
knife 칼(조각칼)
perfect 완벽한

Geppetto lived by himself in a village.
제페토는 어느 한 마을에서 혼자 살고 있었습니다.

This wood is perfect. I will make a new puppet with this wood.
완벽한 나무군. 이 나무로 새 꼭두각시 인형을 만들어야지.

Geppetto went home and began to carve the wood. He made the head with two bright eyes, a pointed nose and a happy mouth. Then he carved the body. He carved two arms, two hands, two legs and two feet. Geppetto was a very good puppet maker. The arms and legs moved easily. Even the head moved up and down, and side to side. Geppetto was very happy with his new puppet.

go(-went-gone) home 집에 가다
begin(-began-begun) to
 …하기 시작하다
make(-made-made) 만들다
bright 빛나는, 생기있는

pointed 뾰족한
move 움직이다
even …조차도
up and down 위아래로
side and side 좌우로, 옆으로

He made the head with two bright eyes, a pointed nose and a happy mouth. 그는 초롱초롱한 두 눈과 뾰족한 코, 미소짓는 입을 한 머리부분을 만들었습니다.

Even the head moved up and down, and side to side.
머리도 위아래와 양옆으로 움직였습니다.

This is my best work. I will call him Pinocchio. He almost looks like a real boy. I wish he was a real boy. I am lonely by myself.

Geppetto did not know it, but a wishing star was in the sky. The wishing star heard his wish. Suddenly, the puppet began to move.

Hello.

Oh, my goodness! You are alive. It's magic.

Is that my name? Am I called Magic?

No, no. Your name is Pinocchio. You are a wooden puppet.

Are you my father?

Well, I made you. So I guess I am.

call (…이라고)이름짓다, 칭하다
look like …인 것 같다
real boy 진짜 사내아이
lonely 외로운, 고독한
wishing 소망을 이루어주는

Oh, my goodness! 이런, 세상에
alive 살아있는
wooden 나무로 만든, 목제의
so 그래서, 그러므로
guess 짐작하다, 추측하다

Geppetto did not know it, but a wishing star was in the sky.
제페토는 하늘에 소원을 들어주는 별이 있다는 사실을 몰랐습니다.

Is that my name? Am I called Magic?
그게 제 이름인가요? 절 매직이라고 부르나요?

Geppetto loved Pinocchio, and Pinocchio loved Geppetto. One day, Geppetto came home late. He was shivering from the cold.

Papa, where is your coat?

I sold it to buy this spelling book for you. Now you can go to school. You can learn to read and write like a real boy.

But Papa, you need your coat. It is cold outside. You are so good to me. I will work hard at school. I will be the best boy in the world. You will be proud of me.

~~~~~~•~~~~~~

I sold it to buy this spelling book for you.
널 위해 이 철자책을 사려고 그 코트를 팔았단다.

You are so good to me. I will work hard at school.
아빠는 제게 너무 잘해 주세요. 학교에서 열심히 공부할게요.

love 사랑하다
come(-came-come) home late
  늦게 귀가하다
shiver from the cold
  추워서 벌벌 떨다
sell(-sold-sold) 팔다
spelling book 철자책

learn 배우다
like …처럼
outside 밖에서
good 친절한
work hard 부지런히 공부하다
be proud of
  …을 자랑스럽게 여기다

The next day, Pinocchio took the book and went to school. He was very excited.

Today I will learn to read. Tomorrow I will learn to write. The next day I will learn my numbers. Soon I will be smart enough to earn money. Then I will buy Papa a new coat.

the next day 그 다음 날
go to school 학교에 가다
take(-took-taken) 가져가다
be excited 흥분하다
write (글을)쓰다

soon 곧, 머지않아
smart 영리한, 현명한
enough to …하여도 될 만큼 충분히 …할
earn money 돈을 벌다

The next day, Pinocchio took the book and went to school.
그 다음 날, 피노키오는 책을 들고 학교에 갔습니다.

Soon I will be smart enough to earn money.
머지않아 나는 돈을 벌 수 있을 만큼 똑똑해질 거야.

But on his way to school, Pinocchio saw a big sign. There was a puppet show in town! Pinocchio wanted to see the show. He wanted to see what other puppets were like. He walked up to the ticket man.

- I want to see the show, but I don't have any money.
- Well, what do you have?
- I have a spelling book.
- Give me your spelling book. Then you can see the show.

on one's way to
　　…으로 가는 길[도중]에
see(-saw-seen) 보다
sign 표지, 게시판
puppet show 꼭두각시 인형극

want to …하기를 원하다
what … like
　　어떠한 …사람[것]일까?
walk up to …에게 다가가다
any (부정문에서)조금도, 전혀

But on his way to school, Pinocchio saw a big sign.
하지만 피노키오는 학교로 가는 길에 큰 안내판을 보았습니다.

He wanted to see what other puppets were like.
그는 다른 꼭두각시 인형들은 어떻게 생겼는지 보고 싶었습니다.

Pinocchio gave the man the spelling book. He forgot the promise he made to Geppetto. He went in and sat down. The show was about to begin. The puppets came out onto the stage. They sang and danced to happy music. Pinocchio was very excited. He was so excited, that he jumped up onto the stage. He was interrupting the show. The people in the audience began to get angry.

On with the show!

I want my money back!

Get that strange puppet off the stage!

He forgot the promise he made to Geppetto.
그는 제페토와 한 약속을 잊어버렸습니다.

He was so excited, that he jumped up onto the stage.
그는 너무 흥분해서 무대 위로 뛰어올라 갔습니다.

The people in the audience began to get angry.
관중 속의 사람들이 화를 내기 시작했습니다.

forget(-forgot-forgotten) 잊다
make a promise 약속을 하다
go(went-gone) in 안으로 들어가다
sit(-sat-sat) down 앉다, 자리잡다
be about to 지금 막 …하려고 하다
stage 무대
sing(-sang-song) 노래하다

dance to the music
　장단에 맞추어 춤추다
interrupt 방해하다
audience 관중, 관객
get angry 화를 내다
back 돌려주다

The manager saw that the show had stopped. When he saw that the crowd was angry, he became angry too. He grabbed one of the puppet masters.

Your show is a disaster. I am losing money. I will burn your puppets for firewood!

Please, sir, burn me for firewood instead. It was all my fault. I interrupted the show. I sold my spelling book, and I should be in school now. I am a bad puppet. Burn me instead.

You are willing to become firewood to save the other puppets? You are a good and brave boy! I will not burn the other puppets, and I will not burn you. Here. Take this money and buy another spelling book.

manager 지배인
crowd 군중
grab 붙잡다
disaster 실패작
master 고용주, 소유자
lose money 손해를 보다
burn 태우다

firewood 장작
instead 대신에
fault 잘못, 실수
be willing to 기꺼이 …하다
save 구하다
brave 용감한

The manager saw that the show had stopped.
지배인은 인형극이 중단된 것을 봤습니다.

It was all my fault. 그건 모두 제 잘못이에요.

You are willing to become firewood to save the other puppets?
넌 다른 인형들을 구하기 위해서 기꺼이 장작이 되겠다는 거니?

Comprehension

Checkup I

I True or False

1. Geppetto lived in a village.
2. The puppet's name was Magic.
3. Geppetto and Pinocchio loved each other.
4. The ticket man let Pinocchio see the show for free.
5. The puppet show manager gave Pinocchio a job.

II Multiple Choice

1. Why was Geppetto lonely?
    a. Because his wife died.
    b. Because he didn't have any friends.
    c. Because he was crazy.

2. Who heard Geppetto's wish?
    a. Pinocchio heard it.
    b. A puppet master heard it.
    c. A wishing start heard it.

3. **Why did Geppetto sell his coat?**

   a. To buy a spelling book.
   b. To buy food.
   c. Because it was warm, and he didn't need his coat.

4. **What did the audience think when Pinocchio interrupted the show?**

   a. They were excited.
   b. They were angry.
   c. They loved Pinocchio.

5. **What did the puppet show manager think of Pinocchio?**

   a. He thought he should be in school.
   b. He thought he was a bad puppet.
   c. He thought he was good and brave.

Comprehension

Checkup I

III **Fill in the Blanks - use the words in the word bank**
(each word is used once)

any	carve	day	home	like
piece	puppets	read	see	wanted

1. One _____, he found a beautiful _____ of wood.

2. Geppetto went _____ and began to _____ the wood.

3. You can learn to _____ and write _____ a real boy.

4. He _____ to see what other _____ were like.

5. I want to _____ the show, but I don't have _____ money.

28 Pinocchio

IV **Draw a line to connect the first half of each sentence with the second half:**

A	B
He carved two arms, two hands,	and went to school.
Geppetto did not know it,	and I will not burn you.
Pinocchio took the book	but a wishing star was in the sky.
I sold my spelling book,	two legs and two feet.
I will not burn the other puppets,	and I should be in school now.

Chapter 2

MP3

Pinocchio went on his way. He wanted to be a good boy. He was very excited, because now he had five pieces of gold.

 I'm rich! I'm rich! Now I can buy a new spelling book, and I can buy Papa a new coat. This is my lucky day.

But a fox and a cat were hiding behind a bush.

go(-went-gone) on one's way
  길을 계속 가다
be a good boy 착한 아이가 되다
excited 흥분된

five pieces of 다섯 개의…
lucky day 운좋은 날
hide 숨다
behind a bush 덤불 뒤에

~~~~~●~~~~~

He was very excited, because now he had five pieces of gold.
이제 그는 금화 다섯 닢을 갖게 되어 매우 흥분되었습니다.

I'm rich! Now I can buy a new spelling book, and I can buy Papa a new coat. 난 부자야! 이제 새 철자책을 살 수도 있고, 아빠한테 새 코트도 사 드릴 수 있어.

They were waiting to trick Pinocchio.

He won't be rich for long.

Soon that money will be ours.

The fox and the cat stepped out onto the road.

Hello Pinocchio. You poor, cold father sent us to find you.

I know I was bad today. But I'm not going to be bad any more. I am going to make my Papa rich! He will be proud of me.

be waiting to
　…하려고 기다리고 있다
won't　will not의 축약형
for long　오랫동안
step out　발걸음을 내딛다

onto the road　도로상으로
send(-sent-sent)　보내다
be going to　…할 예정이다
any more　(부정문에서)
　더 이상, 이제는

He won't be rich for long.　그의 부가 그리 오래가지는 못 할 거야.

I know I was bad today. But I'm not going to be bad any more.
내가 오늘 못된 아이였다는 거 알아. 하지만 더 이상 못된 아이가 되지 않을 거야.

We know how you can make him even richer. Come with us. We'll show you how to plant your gold in the Field of Miracles.

Then, instead of five gold pieces, you will have a whole tree full of gold!

Pinocchio listened to the cat and the fox. He liked the idea of growing gold pieces. Then he could make his Papa really rich. He followed the cat and the fox. They walked for a very long time.

It is a long way to the Field of Miracles, but my Papa will be happy when he sees all the gold I will bring him.

We'll show you how to plant your gold in the Field of Miracles.
우리가 기적의 들판에 네 금을 어떻게 심는지 가르쳐 줄 게.

It is a long way to the Field of Miracles, but my Papa will be happy when he sees all the gold I will bring him.
기적의 들판으로 가는 길은 멀구나. 하지만 내가 가져다 드릴 수많은 금을 보시면 아빠도 기뻐하실 거야.

even (비교급과 함께)더욱 더, 한층
show 가르쳐주다, 보여 주다
plant (땅에)심다
field of miracle 기적의 들판
instead of …대신에
whole 전체의, 모든

full of …으로 가득 찬
growing 자라는
follow 따라가다
for a long time 오랫동안
bring 가져가다

Let me carry your gold pieces. I will keep them safe for you.

No, that's OK. I will keep them myself.

Didn't you hear my friend? He said you should give him the gold pieces.

We must not let you lose the money. Think of your poor, dear papa.

Thank you, but I think I will keep my gold pieces.

let …하게 하다
carry 지니다, 운반하다
keep 보관하다, 맡아두다
that's OK 괜찮아요
oneself 스스로, 몸소

say(-said-said) 말하다
should(=must) …해야 하다
think of …을 생각하다
dear 사랑하는, 사랑스러운

I will keep them safe for you. 널 위해 안전하게 보관해 둘 게.

We must not let you lose the money. Think of your poor, dear papa. 우린 네가 그 돈을 잃어버리지 않도록 해야 해. 네가 사랑하는 가엾은 아버지를 생각해 보렴.

Suddenly, the fox picked Pinocchio up. He turned him upside down and began to shake him. He was trying to find the gold.

- He's lost them already! There's nothing here.

- Check his mouth. He may be hiding them.

- Ouch! His wooden head is hard. I cannot open his mouth.

- Let's tie him to a tree. We'll go eat dinner and come back for him later.

- Good idea. Maybe then he'll give us the gold.

He turned him upside down and began to shake him.
그리고는 거꾸로 들고 흔들기 시작했습니다.

Check his mouth. He may be hiding them.
입 안을 살펴 봐. (금을) 입 안에 숨겼을 지도 몰라.

pick up 들어올리다
turn upside down
   뒤집다, 거꾸로 하다
begin(-began-begun) to shake
   흔들기 시작하다
try to …하려고 하다
lose(-lost-lost) 잃다

already 이미
nothing 아무것도
check 확인하다
may …일지도 모르다
Ouch! (의성어)아얏, 아이쿠
tie 묶다
come back 돌아오다

So the fox and the cat left poor Pinocchio there all by himself. Nearby lived the Blue Fairy. She saw Pinocchio tied to the tree. She sent her falcon to help him.

Falcon, fly to that puppet tied to the tree. Break the rope with your beak and lay him gently on the ground.
Then I will send a carriage for him.

leave(-left-left) 남겨 두다
nearby 가까이에, 근처에
fairy 요정
falcon 매
break the rope 줄을 끊다

beak (새의)부리
lay on the ground 지면에 눕히다
gently 조심스럽게
carriage 마차

~~~~~~~•~~~~~~~

Falcon, fly to that puppet tied to the tree. Break the rope with your beak and lay him gently on the ground. 매야, 나무에 묶여있는 저 꼭두각시 인형에게로 날아가거라. 네 부리로 밧줄을 끊고 조심해서 그를 땅 위에 뉘어 놓거라.

The falcon did exactly what the Blue Fairy asked. Then her carriage brought Pinocchio back to her house. When he arrived, he did not look very good.

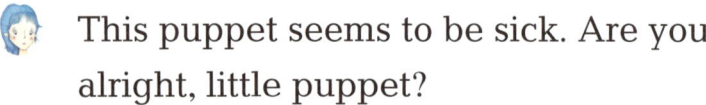 This puppet seems to be sick. Are you alright, little puppet?

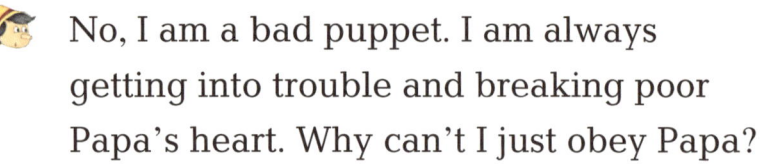 No, I am a bad puppet. I am always getting into trouble and breaking poor Papa's heart. Why can't I just obey Papa?

exactly 정확하게, 바로
ask 부탁하다, 요구하다
arrive 도착하다
seem …처럼 보이다
sick 병든

alright(=all right) 무사한, 괜찮은
get into trouble 말썽을 부리다
break one's heart 몹시 실망시 키다, 비탄에 잠기게 하다
obey 말을 잘 듣다, 복종하다

The falcon did exactly what the Blue Fairy asked.
매는 푸른 요정이 말한 그대로 했습니다.

Why can't I just obey Papa?
왜 전 아빠 말씀을 잘 듣지 않는 걸까요?

🧑 Now, now. Why don't you tell me how you got into all this trouble?

🪵 Papa wants me to be like a real boy. He sold his winter coat to buy me a spelling book. But I sold the spelling book to see a show. I interrupted the show and got into trouble. The show manager was very nice to me. He gave me money to buy a new spelling book. Then a fox and a cat told me about the Field of Miracles. They said that I can plant my gold there, and a tree full of gold will grow.

🧑 Where are the gold pieces? Do you still have them?

Why don't you …? (제안·권유)
 …하는 게 어때요, …하지 않겠어요
get into trouble 곤경에 빠지다
sell(-sold-sold) 팔다
spelling book 철자책
interrupt 방해하다

manager 지배인
be nice to …에게 상냥하다
give(-gave-given) 주다
tell(-told-told) 말하다
plant (땅에 …을)심다
grow 자라다

Now, now. Why don't you tell me how you got into all this trouble?
저런, 저런. 어떻게 해서 이러한 곤경에 빠지게 되었는지 내게 얘기해 주지 않겠니?

Where are the gold pieces? Do you still have them?
그 금화는 어디 있니? 네가 아직 가지고 있니?

Pinocchio did not want to tell the Blue Fairy where his gold was. He remembered how the fox and the cat tried to trick him. He did not trust her.

Well...I...uh...I lost them in the woods.

Suddenly, Pinocchio's nose grew.

Then I will send my dog to find them for you. He finds everything that is lost in the woods.

Oh, wait! I remember now. I...I swallowed them.

remember 기억하다
trick 속이다
trust 믿다, 신용하다
lose(-lost-lost) 잃다

grow(-grew-grown) 자라다
everything 모든 것
swallow 삼키다

Pinocchio did not want to tell the Blue Fairy where his gold was.
피노키오는 푸른 요정에게 금이 어디 있는지 말하고 싶지 않았습니다.

He finds everything that is lost in the woods.
그 개는 숲에서 잃어버린 걸 모두 찾아낸단다.

Again Pinocchio's nose grew. The Blue Fairy laughed.

- Hey, what are you laughing at?
- I'm laughing at your nose. You see, it grows every time you tell a lie.
- Okay, I will tell you the truth. I hid the gold pieces in my mouth. Now they are in my pocket.

laugh at …을 보고 웃다, 비웃다
You see 아시다시피, 있잖아요
every time …할 때마다
tell a lie 거짓말하다

truth 사실, 진실
hide(-hid-hidden) 숨기다
in my pocket 내 호주머니 안에

Hey, what are you laughing at? 뭘 보고 웃는 거죠?

You see, it grows every time you tell a lie.
너도 알다시피 네 코가 거짓말을 할 때마다 커지잖니.

Then Pinocchio's nose went back to its normal size.

Thank you Blue Fairy, but I must go now. I need to find the Field of Miracles so that I can plant my coins. Then I will be rich, and I will be able to take care of Papa.

Pinocchio, it is foolish to plant your gold coins. Money does not grow on trees. Hard work is the only way to make your riches grow.

But I have to try. Good bye, Blue Fairy.

Then I will be rich, and I will be able to take care of Papa.
그러면 전 부자가 되어 아빠를 돌봐드릴 수 있을 거예요.

Hard work is the only way to make your riches grow.
열심히 일하는 것이 부자가 될 수 있는 유일한 방법이란다.

go(-went-gone) back
　원래로 돌아가다
normal size 보통 크기
be able to …할 수 있다

take care of …을 돌보다
foolish 바보같은, 어리석은
hard work 열심히 일하는 것
have to …해야 하다

So Pinocchio once again set out to plant his gold coins in the Field of Miracles. He walked and walked until he came to a sign. The sign said "Field of Miracles straight ahead". Pinocchio ran down the road. When he finally reached the field, he dug holes in the dirt and planted his coins. After his long walk, Pinocchio was tired. He fell asleep under a tree and waited for his money to grow.

once again 다시 한 번
set out 출발하다, 길을 떠나다
sign 안내판, 표지판
straight ahead 앞으로 곧장
run(ran-run) down 뛰어 내려가다
finally 마침내, 드디어

reach 도착하다
dug 파다
hole 구멍
in the dirt 땅에
fall(-fell-fallen) asleep 잠이 들다
wait for …을 기다리다

The sign said "Field of Miracles straight ahead".
그 표지판에는 "기적의 들판, 직진"이라고 쓰여 있었습니다.

When he finally reached the field, he dug holes in the dirt and planted his coins. 마침내 들판에 도착한 피노키오는 땅에 구멍을 파고나서 금화를 심었습니다.

What Pinocchio did not know was that the cat and the fox had secretly followed him there.

- I knew if we waited long enough, we would get his gold.
- Yeah, I can't believe that puppet really thought money grew on trees.
- Come on. Let's get his money and get out of here.

secretly 몰래, 숨어서
follow 따라오다
know(-knew-known) 알다
enough 필요한 만큼, 충분히

think(-thought-thought) 생각하다
Come on (독촉·간청)자, 빨리 빨리
get out of …에서 벗어나다
　　　　　 …범위 밖으로 가다

What Pinocchio did not know was that the cat and the fox had secretly followed him there. 피노키오는 고양이와 여우가 피노키오 몰래 그곳까지 쫓아왔다는 걸 전혀 몰랐습니다.

Come on. Let's get his money and get out of here.
자, 그의 돈을 가지고 어서 이곳을 떠나자.

Comprehension
Checkup II

I True or False

1. The fox and the cat wanted to take Pinocchio home.
2. Pinocchio believed the fox and the cat.
3. The fox and the cat tied Pinocchio to a tree.
4. The Blue Fairy sent a carriage to bring Pinocchio to her house.
5. Pinocchio could not find the Field of Miracles.

II Multiple Choice

1. What did Pinocchio want to buy for his Papa?
   a. He wanted to buy a new spelling book.
   b. He wanted to buy a new coat.
   c. He wanted to buy a new puppet.

2. Why did Pinocchio want to go to the Field of Miracles?
   a. Because he wanted to grow a tree of gold.
   b. Because Geppetto was waiting for him there.
   c. Because he could buy a spelling book there.

3. **What happened to Pinocchio when he told a lie?**

   a. Nothing happened to him.

   b. He turned into firewood.

   c. His nose grew.

4. **Where did Pinocchio hide his gold?**

   a. He hid it in his mouth.

   b. He hid it in his shoe.

   c. He hid it in the Blue Fairy's house.

5. **What happened after Pinocchio planted his gold?**

   a. The gold grew into a tree of money.

   b. The fox and the cat took the money.

   c. The gold turned into beans.

Comprehension

Checkup II

III **Fill in the Blanks - use the words in the word bank**
(each word is used once)

| back | even | getting | go | heart |
| know | make | shake | side | work |

1. We _____ how you can make him _____ richer.

2. He turned him up _____ down and began to _____ him.

3. We'll _____ eat dinner and come _____ for him later.

4. I am always _____ into trouble and breaking poor Papa's _____.

5. Hard _____ is the only way to _____ your riches grow.

IV **Draw a line to connect the first half of each sentence with the second half:**

A	B
The fox and the cat •	• was hard.
Pinocchio's wooden head •	• finds everything lost in the woods.
The Blue Fairy •	• wanted to get Pinocchio's money.
The Blue Fairy's dog •	• does not grow on trees.
Money •	• sent her falcon to help Pinocchio.

Chapter 3

The next morning, Pinocchio woke up. He ran to the place where he'd planted his coins. But when he got there, he saw that his money was all gone. Sadly, he returned home empty-handed. But something was very strange when he got home.

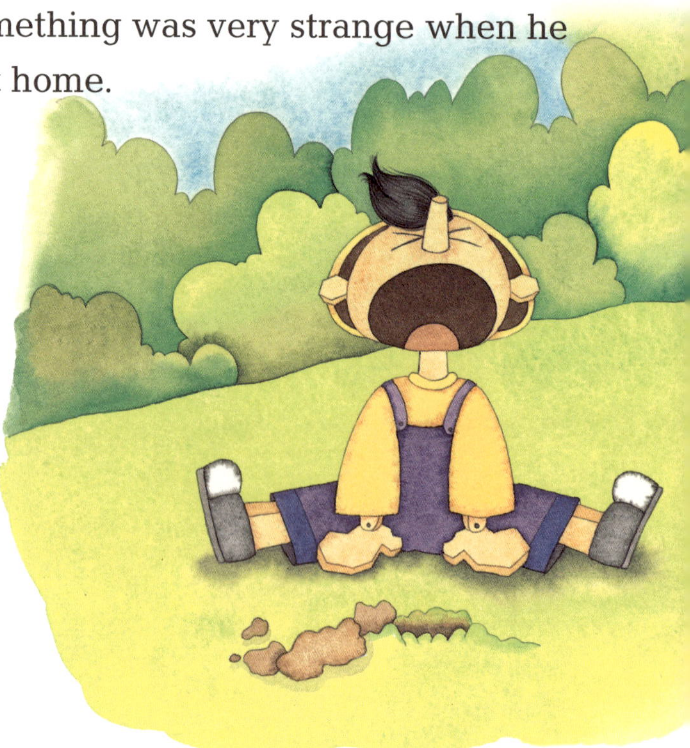

next morning 다음 날 아침
wake(-woke-waken) up 일어나다
run(-ran-run) 달리다
get(-got-gotten) 도착하다
all gone 모두 없어진

sadly 애처롭게
return 돌아가다
empty-handed 빈손으로
strange 이상한

He ran to the place where he'd planted his coins.
그는 금화를 심은 장소로 뛰어갔습니다.

But something was very strange when he got home.
그러나 그가 집에 도착하고 보니 뭔가 매우 이상했습니다.

Hey, the door is locked. Papa! Papa! I have come home. Let me in.

A neighbor was standing outside. He called to Pinocchio.

You are wasting your breath. You were gone so long. Geppetto built a boat and set out to sea to find you.

Oh dear! What have I done now? Maybe if I hurry I can find him.

Hey (놀람·주의)이런, 어이
lock (자물쇠가)잠기다
let me in 들여보내 주세요
neighbor 이웃
stand outside 밖에 서다
call to 부르다

waste one's breath
  쓸데없는 말을 하다
so long 너무 오래
build(-built-built) 만들다, 짓다
set out 출발하다, 길을 떠나다
dear (놀람)저런, 어머나

You were gone so long. 넌 너무 오랫동안 나가 있었어.

Oh dear! What have I done now? Maybe if I hurry I can find him.
오, 저런! 내가 무슨 짓을 한 거지? 서두르면 아빠를 찾을 수 있을 지도 몰라.

Pinocchio quickly ran to the seashore. But he was too late. Geppetto was already gone. Pinocchio saw some sailors. He ran up to them.

Excuse me. Did you see an old man sail away from here?

Yes, we did. We saw him get swallowed up by a huge fish. It was so sad.

What will I do? Where shall I go now that Papa is gone? I will ask the Blue Fairy for help.

We saw him get swallowed up by a huge fish.
우린 거대한 물고기가 그를 삼켜버리는 걸 보았단다.

What will I do? Where shall I go now that Papa is gone?
난 어떻게 하지? 아빠가 돌아가셨으니 난 이제 어디로 가야 하지?

quickly 재빨리
seashore 바닷가
too late 너무 늦은
already 이미, 벌써
sailor 선원
run(-ran-run) up to …으로 뛰어가다

Excuse me 실례합니다
sail 항해하다
swallow 삼키다
huge 커다란
shall …일[할]까요
ask for help 도움을 청하다

Sadly, Pinocchio went to the house of the Blue Fairy and begged her to let him in.

Blue Fairy, may I please stay with you? I will work hard. I will clean the house. I will carry the water. I will do anything.

You will go to school and study hard! Yes, you may stay with me, Pinocchio.

I promise, this time I will obey.

---

sadly 애처롭게
beg 애원하다, 부탁하다
let in 들이다, 들여보내다
May I …?
    …해도 좋을[괜찮을]까요?
stay with 머무르다

clean 깨끗이 하다
anything 무엇이든
study hard 열심히 공부하다
this time 이번에는
obey 말을 잘 듣다, 복종하다

Sadly, Pinocchio went to the house of the Blue Fairy and begged her to let him in. 슬픔에 빠진 피노키오는 푸른 요정의 집으로 가서 들여보내 달라고 애원했습니다.

You will go to school and study hard! Yes, you may stay with me, Pinocchio. 학교에 가서 열심히 공부한다구! 그래, 그럼 나와 함께 우리집에 머물러도 좋아, 피노키오.

Pinocchio

So Pinocchio went to school, and he studied very hard. Soon he became the hardest working student in the whole school. But the other boys got jealous because Pinocchio was doing so well.

That puppet is making us all look like dummies.

Yeah. Let's teach him not to be so smart.

When recess starts, let's beat him up.

OK!

soon 곧, 머지않아
hardest (hard의 최상급)가장 열심히
whole school 전학교
jealous 시기하는, 시샘하는
so well 너무 잘
look like …인 것 같다

dummy (속어)바보, 멍청이
teach 가르치다
smart 영리한, 현명한
recess 쉬는 시간, 휴식
beat up 호되게 때리다

~~~~~~~●~~~~~~~

But the other boys got jealous because Pinocchio was doing so well. 하지만 다른 아이들은 피노키오가 너무 잘 해서 그를 시샘했습니다.

When recess starts, let's beat him up.
쉬는 시간에 녀석을 호되게 때려 주자.

When Pinocchio came outside for recess, the boys surrounded him and began fighting with him. They hit him in the head, punched him on his arms, and kicked him on his legs.

Trying to be smarter than a real boy? We'll show you.

Yeah, you can't be smarter than a real boy.

Ouch! His head is as hard as wood. I hurt my hand!

Ow, ow, ow! I hurt my foot on his leg.

We give up. Let's be friends instead.

They all shook hands and agreed to be friends.

surround 에워싸다, 둘러싸다
fight 싸우다
hit 치다, 때리다
punch 주먹으로 치다
kick 발로 차다
show 보여주다
Ouch! (의성어)아얏, 아이쿠

as …처럼[만큼]
hurt 아프다, 아프게 하다
give up 포기하다
be friend 친구가 되다
shake(-shook-shaken) hands
  악수하다
agree 동의하다

When Pinocchio came outside for recess, the boys surrounded him and began fighting with him. 피노키오가 쉬는 시간에 밖으로 나오자, 아이들이 그를 에워싸고 싸우기 시작했습니다.

Ouch! His head is as hard as wood. I hurt my hand!
아얏! 이 녀석 머리는 나무처럼 딱딱해. 내 손이 아퍼.

That night, Pinocchio told the Blue Fairy about what happened at school that day. He really began to think about what the boys said about him not being real.

- I wish I were a real boy, instead of a funny, wooden puppet.

- If you are good and brave and keep working hard, someday you may have your wish.

- Oh, I will work hard. I promise.

He really began to think about what the boys said about him not being real. 그는 아이들이 자신에게 진짜 아이가 아니라고 한 말에 대해 진지하게 생각하기 시작했습니다.

If you are good and brave and keep working hard, someday you may have your wish. 네가 착하고 용감해진다면 그리고 계속 공부를 열심히 한다면 언젠가는 네 소원이 이루어질 거란다.

that night 그 날 밤
funny 기묘한, 우스운
wooden 나무로 만든, 목제의
brave 용감한

keep (어떤 상태를)계속하다, 유지하다
someday 언젠가는
have one's wish
　　소망이 이루어지다

But the very next day, Pinocchio forgot his promise. On his way to school, he saw one of his new friends.

- Hey, Pinocchio! Know where I'm going?
- No. Where?
- I'm going to a place where you never have to work, just play and have fun all day long. Want to come too?
- Well, I shouldn't. I have test today.
- Come on. It will be great. And it will be much more fun than a boring test.

I'm going to a place where you never have to work, just play and have fun all day long. 전혀 일할 필요가 없는 곳에 가는 중이야. 단지 하루 종일 즐겁게 놀기만 하면 되는 곳이지.

And it will be much more fun than a boring test.
그리고 그건 따분한 시험보다는 훨씬 재미있을 거야.

very 바로 그
on one's way
  …으로 가는 길[도중]에
never 결코[전혀] …하다
all day long 종일토록

have fun 재미있게 놀다
much more … than ~
  ~보다 훨씬 …한
boring 따분한, 지루한

Where did you say it was?

It's called the Land of Pleasures. Here's the coach to take us there right now. Make up your mind, Pinocchio.

A land where there's no work and all play? Okay, I'll come!

Hey, Coachman. Two seats for my friend and me.

Sorry, I only have one seat left. Your friend can ride on the back of one of the donkeys.

Pinocchio ran up to a donkey and got on its back.

pleasure 즐거움, 오락
coach 마차
right now 지금 당장
make up one's mind
    결심하다, 결단을 내리다
coachman 마부
seat 좌석
leave(-left-left) 남다
ride on the back 등에 올라타다
donkey 당나귀

A land where there's no work and all play?
일하지 않고 놀기만 하는 나라란 말이지?

Two seats for my friend and me.
저와 제 친구가 앉을 두 좌석을 부탁해요.

Pinocchio ran up to a donkey and got on its back.
피노키오는 당나귀에게로 달려가 그(당나귀)의 등에 올라탔습니다.

 This is going to be so much fun. All that studying was hurting my head anyway.

Poor fool.

Did you just speak, donkey?

Yes, I spoke. And I cry, as you too will cry someday. You will be sorry you left school and the ones you love.

Humph! What does a donkey know?

anyway 어쨌든, 아무튼
fool 바보, 어리석은 사람
speak(-spoke-spoken) 말하다
as …와 같이

someday 언젠가, 훗날
sorry 후회하는
humph! (의심·조소)흥, 흠

All that studying was hurting my head anyway.
아무튼 공부만 하면 머리가 아팠거든.

You will be sorry you left school and the ones you love.
넌 학교와 네가 사랑하는 사람들을 떠난 걸 후회하게 될 거야.

When the coach arrived at the wonderful Land of Pleasures, Pinocchio was so happy to join the fun that he forgot all about work. He even forgot about the Blue Fairy and poor Geppetto. He ate candy, played games, rode rides, and never did any work. For many months, all he did was play and play and play.

join 참가하다, 축에 끼다
ride(-rode-ridden) 타다[동사]
 (유원지등의)탈것 [명사]

never do any work
 전혀 아무 일도 하지 않다
for many months 여러 달 동안

Pinocchio was so happy to join the fun that he forgot all about work.
일에 대해서는 완전히 잊고 마음껏 즐길 수 있어서 매우 행복했습니다.

For many months, all he did was play and play and play.
여러 달 동안 그가 한 일이라고는 놀고, 놀고, 또 논 것 밖에 없었습니다.

Then one morning Pinocchio looked in the mirror. He was frightened by what he saw.

Oh no! Look at my ears! They look like donkey ears.

A few minutes later, Pinocchio's friend entered the room. He had donkey ears too. The coachman was with him.

Hey, you have ears like a donkey.

So do you.

That's right. Boys who play all day, instead of studying turn into donkeys.

look in 잠깐 들여다보다
frighten 소스라쳐 놀라게 하다
look at …을 보다
a few minutes later
　몇 분 후, 잠시 후

enter 들어오다
so …도 역시[또한]
That's right 그렇소, 맞았소
instead of …대신에
turn into 변하다

He was frightened by what he saw.
그는 거울에 비친 모습을 보고 깜짝 놀랐습니다.

Boys who play all day, instead of studying turn into donkeys.
하루 종일 공부하지 않고 놀기만 하는 아이들은 당나귀로 변한단다.

- What's happening to us?
- I don't know, but I can't stand up straight anymore.
- We really are turning into donkeys!
- I guess you two are ready to be sold at the market.
- The market? What do you mean?
- What did you think I brought you to this land for? To play the rest of your lives? Now that you are donkeys, I will sell you in the market. You will bring me lots of money.

happen 일어나다, 발생하다
stand up straight 똑바로 서다
anymore (부정문에서)이제는
be ready to …할 준비가 되다
market 시장

What do you mean?
　　그게 무슨 말이죠?
bring(-brought-brought) 데려오다
rest of one's life 여생

~~~~~~●~~~~~~

What's happening to us?　우리에게 무슨 일이 일어나고 있는 거지?

What did you think I brought you to this land for? To play the rest of your lives?　내가 무엇 때문에 너희들을 이 곳으로 데려왔다고 생각하니? 평생 마음껏 놀게 해 주기 위해서?

Comprehension

Checkup III

I **True or False**

1. Pinocchio told Geppetto that he lost his gold.
2. Geppetto was swallowed by a huge bird.
3. The boys at school decided to be friends with Pinocchio.
4. A circus owner bought Pinocchio at the market.
5. The sea water turned Pinocchio into a real boy.

II **Multiple Choice**

1. **Why did Geppetto set out to sea?**
   a. To visit the Blue Fairy.
   b. To go to the Land of Pleasures.
   c. To find Pinocchio.

2. **Why were the other boys jealous of Pinocchio?**
   a. Because he was a good fighter.
   b. Because he was a good student.
   c. Because he was made of wood.

3. What is special about the Land of Pleasures?

   a. You can play and have fun all day.

   b. You can take a test everyday.

   c. Only wooden puppets can go there.

4. What kind of boys turn into donkeys?

   a. Boys who work all day.

   b. Boys who study all day.

   c. Boys who play all day.

5. What did the coachman say when Pinocchio and boy turned into donkeys?

   a. He will sell them in the market.

   b. He will give them candy.

   c. He will bring them to another land.

Comprehension

Checkup III

III **Fill in the Blanks - use the words in the word bank**
(each word is used once)

| handed | huge | may | night | ones |
| ready | returned | sorry | swallowed | with |

1. Sadly, he _____ home empty-_____.

2. Blue Fairy, _____ I please stay _____ you?

3. You will be _____ you left school and the _____ you love.

4. Pinocchio practiced day and _____, until he was _____ for his first performance.

5. The fish opened its _____ mouth and _____ Pinocchio up.

Pinocchio

IV **Draw a line to connect the first half of each sentence with the second half:**

A	B
The neighbor said to pinocchio that Geppeto wanted	to be a real boy.
The Blue Fairy wanted	to sell donkeys at the market.
The boys at school wanted	to beat up Pinocchio.
Pinocchio wanted	Pinocchio to go to school and study hard.
The coachman wanted	to find Pinocchio.

Chapter 4

The coachman took Pinocchio and his friend to the market. Poor Pinocchio was sold to a circus owner. The circus owner put Pinocchio into a cage.

- Hurry up and eat. We have much to do.

- Hay? Is that all I get to eat?

- What else would you want? You are just a donkey.

- I wish I stayed in school.

- Meal time is over. I didn't buy you just to feed you. Get up! It's time to work.

coachman 마부
take(-took-taken) 데려가다
circus owner 서커스 주인
put into …안에 집어넣다
cage 우리
Hurry up! 서둘러라

have to 점점 더 가까워지다
hay 건초
meal time 식사시간
over 끝나다
feed 먹이를 주다
Get up! 일어나

What else would you want? 뭘 더 바라는 거냐?

Meal time is over. I didn't buy you just to feed you. Get up! It's time to work. 식사 시간이 끝났다. 그저 밥만 먹여 주려고 널 산게 아냐? 일어나! 일할 시간이다.

The circus owner made poor Pinocchio work very hard. He made him perform many dances and jump through a ring of fire. Pinocchio practiced day and night until finally he was ready for his first performance.

 Good evening, ladies and gentlemen! Welcome to the best show in town! Presenting Pinocchio, the famous dancing donkey. Watch him dance! Watch him jump through a ring of fire!

Pinocchio practiced day and night until finally he was ready for his first performance. 피노키오는 밤낮으로 연습을 했고 마침내 첫 공연을 준비하게 되었습니다.

Welcome to the best show in town! Presenting Pinocchio, the famous dancing donkey. 마을 최고의 쇼에 오신 걸 환영합니다. 유명한 춤추는 당나귀, 피노키오를 소개합니다.

perform a dance 춤을 추다
through 통과하여
practice 연습하다
day and night 밤낮으로
be ready for 준비가 되다
performance 공연

ladies and gentlemen!
 신사, 숙녀 여러분
welcome 환영하다
present 소개하다
famous 유명한
watch 지켜보다

The crowd began to cheer. Pinocchio danced well. But when he tried to jump through the ring of fire, his leg got caught.

Oh, my leg is hurt! I can't jump through the ring of fire.

You are no good to me with a hurt leg. I will get rid of you.

The circus owner threw Pinocchio into the sea.

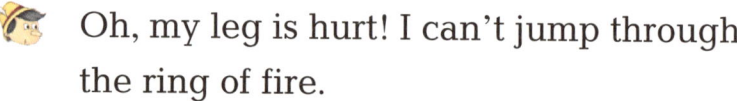

But when he tried to jump through the ring of fire, his leg got caught. 하지만 불붙은 고리를 뛰어서 통과하려고 하자 다리가 걸리고 말았습니다.

You are no good to me with a hurt leg.
다친 다리를 하고서는 내게 아무런 쓸모가 없어.

crowd 군중, 인파
cheer 환호하다
get(got-gotten) caught 걸리다
be no good
　아무 쓸모도 없다, 소용 없다
hurt leg 다친 다리
get rid of 제거하다, 없애다
throw(-threw-thrown) 버리다
into the sea 바다 속에

Pinocchio was glad to have his freedom back, even if he was in the middle of the sea. Then an amazing thing happened. The sea water changed him back to a puppet. He was not a donkey any more. He began swimming back to shore. Suddenly, a giant fish appeared. Pinocchio swam as fast as he could, but the fish opened its huge mouth and swallowed Pinocchio up.

glad 기쁜
freedom 자유
even if 비록 …할 지라도
amazing thing 놀라운 일
change 바뀌다, 변하다
shore 해안가

giant 거대한
swim(swam-swum) 헤엄치다
as … as one can
　될 수 있는 한 …
swallow up 집어삼키다

Pinocchio was glad to have his freedom back, even if he was in the middle of the sea.　피노키오는 비록 바다 한 가운데 있었지만 다시 자유를 찾은 것이 기뻤습니다.

Pinocchio swam as fast as he could, but the fish opened its huge mouth and swallowed Pinocchio up.　피노키오는 될 수 있는 한 빨리 헤엄쳤지만 물고기는 큰 입을 벌리고 피노키오를 집어삼키고 말았습니다.

Everything was dark inside the big fish. But there was a tiny little light in the distance. Pinocchio followed the light, and it led him to an old man. It was Geppetto!

 Papa! It's you!

 Pinocchio, my son! I found you at last.

Oh Papa! I will never, never leave you again!

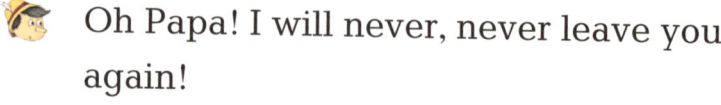 That is too true my son, for we will never escape from this fish.

everything 모든 것
tiny 아주 조그만
light 불빛
in the distance 먼 곳에

lead(-led-led) 이끌다
at last 마침내, 드디어
escape 탈출하다

Pinocchio followed the light, and it led him to an old man.
피노키오는 그 불빛을 따라갔습니다. 그러자 한 나이든 사람이 있는 곳에 이르렀습니다.

That is too true my son, for we will never escape from this fish.
그건 정말 맞구나, 우리는 이 물고기의 뱃속에서 결코 빠져나가지 못할 테니까 말이다.

Just then, Pinocchio heard a noise.

What was that noise?

That was the fish. He is very old, and when he sleeps, he snores.

Look, Papa! He sleeps with his mouth open. Now is the time to escape.

But I am old and weak. I cannot swim all the way to shore.

I will help you. Let's go.

---

just then 바로 그 때
noise 소리, 소음
snore 코를 골다

with one's mouth open
입을 벌린 채
weak (몸이)허약한

What was that noise? 저 소리는 뭐죠?

Look, Papa! He sleeps with his mouth open. Now is the time to escape. 아빠, 보세요! 물고기가 입을 벌린 채로 자요. 지금이 바로 빠져 나갈 기회예요.

Pinocchio put old Geppetto on his back and began swimming to the shore.

It is a long way to the shore, my son. You will be too tired if you carry me all the way.

Don't worry, Papa. I am strong. I can do it.

I still cannot see the shore.

Don't be afraid. I will save you, Papa.

tired 지친, 힘든
carry 데려가다
Don't worry 걱정 마세요

still 아직도
Don't be afraid 무서워하지 마세요
save 구하다

~~~~~~~●~~~~~~~

Pinocchio put old Geppetto on his back and began swimming to the shore. 피노키오는 늙은 제페토를 자신의 등에 태우고 해안가를 향해 헤엄치기 시작했습니다.

You will be too tired if you carry me all the way.
해안가까지 날 데려가려면 네가 너무 지쳐 버릴 거야.

At last, a friendly wave washed Geppetto and Pinocchio up on the shore. Pinocchio was so tired, that he could hardly stand up.

 Come on, Pinocchio. Let's go home.

Leaning on each other, Geppetto and Pinocchio slowly made their way back home. It was so good to be back home again. They were very tired from their long journey. They both went to bed early.

friendly 부드러운
wave 파도
wash (파도에)떠밀리다
hardly 거의 …않다
stand up 서다

lean on …에 의지하다[기대다]
each other 서로
slowly 천천히
journey 여행
go to bed 잠자리에 들다, 자다

Pinocchio was so tired, that he could hardly stand up.
피노키오는 거의 서 있을 수 조차 없을 정도로 매우 지쳐 있었습니다.

Leaning on each other, Geppetto and Pinocchio slowly made their way back home. 제페토와 피노키오는 서로 의지하면서 천천히 집으로 돌아갔습니다.

That night a most wonderful thing happened to Pinocchio. When he woke up the next morning, he had a big surprise.

 Papa! Papa! Look at me! I'm a real boy!

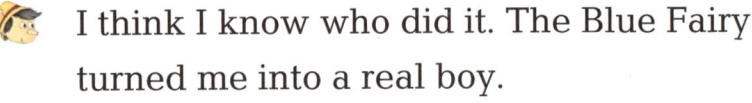 How did this happen? This is the happiest day of my life!

 I think I know who did it. The Blue Fairy turned me into a real boy.

that night 그 날 밤
wake(-woke-waken) up 일어나다
have a big surprise 크게 놀라다

happiest (happy의 최상급)
　　　 가장 행복한
turn into …으로 바꾸다

When he woke up the next morning, he had a big surprise.
다음 날 아침, 잠에서 깬 피노키오는 크게 놀랐습니다.

How did this happen? This is the happiest day of my life!
어떻게 이런 일이? 오늘은 내 인생에서 가장 행복한 날이구나.

Just then the Blue Fairy appeared.

No, Pinocchio. You did it yourself. Last night, you saved Geppetto's life. You swam through the terrible sea, and you did not give up. You proved you weren't a wooden head anymore. You were ready to become a real boy.

I'm so proud of you, Pinocchio.

Thank you, Papa.

Geppetto and Pinocchio danced and celebrated and lived happily ever after.

appear 나타나다
do oneself 스스로 하다
last night 지난 밤
swim(-swam-swum) 헤엄치다

prove 증명하다
celebrate 축하하다
ever after 그 후 내내

You did it yourself. 너 혼자서 그걸 해낸 거란다.

I'm so proud of you, Pinocchio.
피노키오, 난 네가 정말 자랑스럽구나.

Comprehension
Checkup IV

I True or False

1. Pinocchio saw a light inside the fish.
2. The big fish never sleeps.
3. Pinocchio was very tired when they got to shore.
4. As soon as they got home, Geppetto and Pinocchio celebrated.
5. Geppetto was proud of Pinocchio.

II Multiple Choice

1. Who did Pinocchio find in the fish?
    a. He found Geppetto.
    b. He found the Blue Fairy.
    c. He found his friends from school.

2. Why couldn't Geppetto swim to shore?
    a. Because he didn't know how to swim.
    b. Because he was afraid of water.
    c. Because he was old and weak.

3. **How did Pinocchio carry Geppetto to the shore?**

    a. He built a raft.

    b. He put him on his back.

    c. He made a net.

4. **What helped Pinocchio and Geppetto get to shore?**

    a. A helpful fish carried them to shore.

    b. A big ship sailed them to shore.

    c. A friendly wave washed them up on the shore.

5. **Who turned Pinocchio into a real boy?**

    a. The Blue Fairy did.

    b. Pinocchio did.

    c. The wishing star did.

Comprehension

Checkup IV

III **Fill in the Blanks - use the words in the word bank**
(each word is used once)

| again | all | give | happened | happiest |
| life | never | night | through | tired |

1. I will _____, never leave you _____.

2. You will be too _____ if you carry me _____ the way.

3. That _____, a most wonderful thing _____ to Pinocchio.

4. This is the _____ day of my _____.

5. You swam _____ the terrible sea, and you did not _____ up.

정답은 p.117에

IV **Draw a line to connect the words that are opposites of each other:**

A	B
Sell	Work
Remember	Buy
Lose	Strange
Play	Find
Normal	Forget

Comprehension Checkup

Checkup I (26~29p)

I 1. T   2. F   3. T   4. F   5. F

II 1. a   2. c   3. a   4. b   5. c

III
1. day, piece
2. home, carve
3. read, like
4. wanted, puppets
5. see, any

IV

A	B
He carved two arms, two hands,	and went to school.
Geppetto did not know it,	and I will not burn you.
Pinocchio took the book	but a wishing star was in the sky.
I sold my spelling book,	two legs and two feet.
I will not burn the other puppets,	and I should be in school now.

Matches (per connecting lines):
- He carved two arms, two hands, — two legs and two feet.
- Geppetto did not know it, — but a wishing star was in the sky.
- Pinocchio took the book — and went to school.
- I sold my spelling book, — and I should be in school now.
- I will not burn the other puppets, — and I will not burn you.

Pinocchio

Comprehension Checkup

Checkup II (56~59p)

I 1. F 2. T 3. T 4. T 5. F

II 1. b 2. a 3. c 4. a 5. b

III
1. know, even
2. side, shake
3. go, back
4. getting, heart
5. work, make

IV

A	B
The fox and the cat	was hard.
Pinocchio's wooden head	finds everything lost in the woods.
The Blue Fairy	wanted to get Pinocchio's money.
The Blue Fairy's dog	does not grow on trees.
Money	sent her falcon to help Pinocchio.

Comprehension Checkup

Checkup III (86~89p)

I 1. F 2. F 3. T 4. T 5. F

II 1. c 2. b 3. a 4. c 5. a

III
1. returned, handed
2. may, with
3. sorry, ones
4. night, ready
5. huge, swallowed

IV

A	B
The neighbor said to pinocchio that Geppeto wanted	to be a real boy.
The Blue Fairy wanted	to sell donkeys at the market.
The boys at school wanted	to beat up Pinocchio.
Pinocchio wanted	Pinocchio to go to school and study hard.
The coachman wanted	to find Pinocchio.

Comprehension Checkup

Checkup IV (110~113p)

I 1. T 2. F 3. T 4. F 5. T

II 1. a 2. c 3. b 4. c 5. b

III
1. never, again
2. tired, all
3. night, happened
4. happiest, life
5. through, give

IV

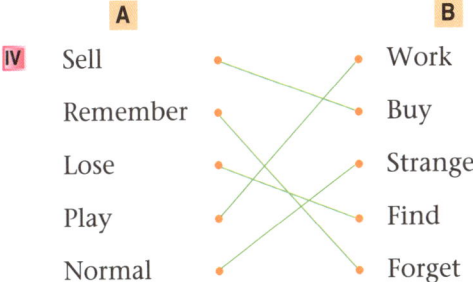

Word List

다음은 이 책에 나오는 단어와 숙어를 수록한 것입니다.
* 표는 중학교 영어 교육 과정의 기본 어휘입니다.

A

a few minutes later	83
agree*	71
alive	15
all day long	75
all gone	61
already	39 / 65
alright	42
amazing thing	97
any*	21
any more	33
anymore	85
anything	66
anyway	79
appear*	108
arrive*	42
as*	71 / 79
as ⋯ as one can	97
ask*	42
ask for help	65
at last	99
audience	23

B

back*	23
be a good boy	31
be able to	51
be about to	23
be excited	18
be friend	71
be going to	33
be nice to	45
be no good	95
be proud of	17
be ready for	93
be ready to	85
be waiting to	33
be willing to	25
beak	41
beat up	69
beg	66
begin to	13

118 Pinocchio

begin to shake	39	come back	39
behind a bush	31	come home late	17
boring	75	Come on	55
brave	25 / 73	crowd*	25 / 95
break one's heart	42		
break the rope	41	**D**	
bright*	13		
bring*	35 / 85	dance to the music	23
build*	63	day and night	93
burn*	25	dear*	37 / 63
by oneself	11	disaster	25
		do oneself	108
C		Don't be afraid	103
		Don't worry	103
cage*	91	donkey	77
call*	15	dug	53
call to	63	dummy	69
carriage	41		
carry*	37 / 103	**E**	
carve	11		
celebrate	108	each other	105
change*	97	earn money	18
check*	39	empty-handed	61
cheer	95	enough*	55
circus owner	91	enough to	18
clean*	66	enter*	83
coach	77	escape	99
coachman	77 / 91	even*	13 / 35

even if	97	forget*	23
ever after	108	freedom*	97 / 105
every time	48	frighten	83
everything	46 / 99	full of*	35
exactly*	42	funny*	73
excited	31		
Excuse me	65		

F

G

fairy	41	gently	41
falcon	41	get*	61
fall asleep	53	get angry	23
famous*	93	get caught	95
fault*	25	get into trouble	42 / 45
feed*	91	get out of	55
field of miracle	35	get rid of	95
fight*	71	Get up!	91
finally*	53	giant	97
find*	11	give*	45
firewood	25	give up	71
five pieces of	31	glad*	97
follow*	35 / 55	go back	51
fool*	79	go home	13
foolish	51	go in	23
for a long time	35	go on one's way	31
for long	33	go to bed	105
for many months	81	go to school	18
		good*	17
		grab	25

grow*	45 / 46
growing	35
guess*	15

H

happen*	85
happiest	107
hard work	51
hardest	69
hardly*	105
have a big surprise	107
have fun	75
have one's wish	73
have to	51 / 91
hay	91
Hey	63
hide*	31 / 48
hit*	71
hole*	53
huge*	65
humph!	79
Hurry up!	91
hurt*	71
hurt leg	95

I

in my pocket	48
in the dirt	53
in the distance	99
instead*	25
instead of	35 / 83
interrupt	23 / 45
into the sea	95

J

jealous	69
join*	81
journey	105
just then	100

K

keep*	37 / 73
kick*	71
knife*	11
know*	55

L

ladies and gentlemen!	93
last night	108

laugh at	48
lay on the ground	41
lead*	99
lean on	105
learn*	17
leave*	41 / 77
let*	37
let in	66
let me in	63
light*	99
like*	17
live in	11
lock*	63
lonely	15
look at	83
look in	83
look like	15 / 69
lose*	39 / 46
lose money	25
love*	17
lucky day	31

M

make*	13
make a promise	23
make up one's mind	77
maker	11
manager	25 / 45
many years ago	11
market*	85
master*	25
may*	39
May I …?	66
meal time	91
move*	13
much more … than ~	75

N

nearby	41
neighbor	63
never*	75
never do any work	81
next morning	61
noise*	100
normal size	51
nothing*	39

O

obey	42 / 66
Oh, my goodness!	15
on one's way	75
on one's way to	21
once again	53

once upon a time	11	**R**	
one day	11	reach*	53
oneself	37	real boy	15
onto the road	33	recess	69
Ouch!	39 / 71	remember*	46
outside*	17	rest of one's life	85
over*	91	return*	61
		ride*	81
P		ride on the back	77
		right now	77
perfect	11	run*	61
perform a dance	93	run down	53
performance	93	run up to	65
pick up	39		
plant*	35 / 45	**S**	
pleasure	77		
pointed	13	sadly	61 / 66
practice*	93	sail	65
present*	93	sailor	65
prove	108	save*	25 / 103
punch	71	say*	37
puppet	11	seashore	65
puppet show	21	seat*	77
put into	91	secretly	55
		see*	21
Q		seem*	42
quickly	65	sell*	17 / 45

send*	33
set out	53 / 63
shake hands	71
shall*	65
shiver from the cold	17
shore	97
should	37
show*	35 / 71
sick*	42
side and side	13
sign*	21 / 53
sing*	23
sit down	23
slowly	105
smart	18 / 69
snore	100
so*	15 / 83
so long	63
so well	69
someday	73 / 79
soon*	18 / 69
sorry*	79
speak*	79
spelling book	17 / 45
stage	23
stand outside	63
stand up	105
stand up straight	85
stay with	66
step out	33
still*	103
straight*	11
straight ahead	53
strange*	61
study hard	66
surround	71
swallow	46 / 65
swallow up	97
swim*	97 / 108

T

take*	18 / 91
take care of	51
teach*	69
tell*	45
tell a lie	48
that night	73 / 107
that's OK	37
That's right	83
the next day	18
think*	55
think of	37
this time	66
through*	93
throw*	95

tie*	39
tiny*	99
tired	103
too late	65
trick	46
trust	46
truth*	48
try to	39
turn into	83 / 107
turn upside down	39

U

up and down	13

V

very*	75
village	11

W

wait for	53
wake up	61 / 107
walk up to	21
want to	21
wash*	105
wast one's breath	63
watch*	93
wave	105
weak*	100
welcome*	93
What do you mean?	85
what … like	21
whole*	35
whole school	69
Why don't you …?	45
wishing	15
with one's mouth open	100
won't	33
wooden	15 / 73
work hard	17
write*	18

Y

You see	48

Story House
17. Pinocchio 피노키오

펴낸이	임 병 업
펴낸곳	(주)월드컴 에듀
등록	2000년 1월 17일
주소	서울특별시 강남구 언주로 120
	인스토피아 빌딩 912호
전화	02)3273-4300(대표)
팩스	02)3273-4303
홈페이지	www.wcbooks.co.kr
이메일	wc4300@wcbooks.co.kr

* 본 교재는 저작권법에 의해 보호를 받는 저작물이므로 무단전재 및 무단복제를 금합니다.